arcola
theatre

We Started to Sing

by Barney Norris

We Started to Sing was first performed at Arcola Theatre,
London, on 19 May 2022

We Started to Sing

Barney Norris

Cast

DAVID	David Ricardo-Pearce
PEGGY	Barbara Flynn
BERT	Robin Soans
FIONA	Naomi Petersen
ROB	George Taylor

Production Team

Director/Writer	Barney Norris
Set and Costume Designer	Frankie Bradshaw
Lighting Designer	Bethany Gupwell
Video Designer	Megan Lucas
Musical Arranger	Timmy Fisher
Sound Designer	Jamie Lu
Costume Supervisor	Olivia Ward
Production Manager	Josephine Tremelling
Stage Manager on Book	Hayley Bowman
Assistant Stage Manager	Emily Compton
ASM Student Placement	Elsie O'Rourke
Dialect Consultant	Mary Howland
Image Design	Rebecca Pitt

Cast and Production Team

Barney Norris (Writer and Director)
Barney Norris is a playwright and novelist. His work has received awards from the International Theatre Institute, the Critics' Circle, the *Evening Standard*, the Society of Authors and the South Bank Sky Arts Times Breakthrough Awards, among others, and been translated into eight languages. His plays include *Visitors*, *Nightfall* and an acclaimed adaptation of Kazuo Ishiguro's *The Remains of the Day*; his novels include *Five Rivers Met on a Wooded Plain*.

David Ricardo-Pearce (DAVID)
David Ricardo-Pearce's theatre credits include *The Lorax* (Old Vic); *Crossing Jerusalem* (Park Theatre); *A Midsummer Night's Dream* (Barbican/Bristol Old Vic); *Kiss me Kate* (Watermill Theatre); *The Big Fellah* (Lyric Hammersmith); *Hamlet*, *Romeo and Juliet*, *The Last Yankee* (Octagon Theatre); *Middlemarch*, *De Monfort* (Orange Tree); *The Sacred Flame* (ETT); *Saint Joan* (National Theatre); *Privates on Parade* (WYP/Birmingham Rep); *The Car Cemetery* (Gate Theatre); *Annie Get Your Gun* (Young Vic); *Alfie*, *Inglorious Technicolour* (Stephen Joseph Theatre); *Anyone Can Whistle* (Jeremy Street Theatre); *Saturday Night*, *The Great Gatsby* (Arts Theatre); *Sweeney Todd* (Trafalgar Studios). His television and film credits include *Traitors*, *Trauma*, *EastEnders*, *The Spa*, *Outnumbered*, *Extras*, *Border Crossing*, *Ma'am* and *Stop Dead*. unitedagents.co.uk/david-ricardo-pearce

Barbara Flynn (PEGGY)
Barbara Flynn's theatre credits include: *Elegy*, *Versailles* (Donmar Warehouse); *High Society* (Old Vic); *The Revengers Tragedy*, *King Lear*, *Antigone*, *Tales from Hollywood*, *Early Days*, *The Philanderer*, *Plunder* (National Theatre); *The Way of the World* (Lyric Theatre Hammersmith); *Agamemnon's children*, *Women of Troy* (Gate Theatre); *Hamlet* (Crucible Theatre); *An Experiment with an Air Pump*, *The Perfectionist*, *Short List* (Hampstead Theatre); *Copenhagen* (Lyceum Theatre Sheffield) and *Vivat Vivat Regina* (Mermaid). Television credits include: *Kate and Koji*, *Doctor Who*, *The Durrells*, *Killing Eve*, *Cranford*, *Pat & Cabbage*, *The Borgias*, *10 Days to War*, *Cracker*, *The Line of Beauty*, *Elizabeth I*, *Malice Aforethought*, *Death in Paradise*, *A Very Peculiar Practice*, *1864*, *Beiderbecke Trilogy*, *The Queen* and *A Family at War*. Film credits include: *The Christmas Candle*, *Cheerful Weather for the Wedding*, *Burlesque Fairy Tales*, *King Lear*, *You're Dead* and *Miss Potter*.

Robin Soans (BERT)
Former work at the Arcola comprises of *Palace of the End*, *Pieces of Vincent* and *Visitors*. He is the author of *Crouch, Touch, Pause, Engage*. Robin has worked extensively in the theatre, including the RSC, the

National, the Royal Court, Hampstead and the Bush. Recent films include *The Queen, Pierrepoint, Victoria and Abdul, Red Juan, Viceroy's House* and *The Princess Switch* franchise.

Naomi Petersen (FIONA)

Naomi Petersen's theatre credits include *Baskerville!* (Mercury Theatre); *The Girl Next Door, Birthdays Past Birthdays Present, Joking Apart, Better off Dead* (Stephen Joseph Theatre); *By Jeeves* (The Old Laundry Theatre); *The Sorcerer's Apprentice* (Ambassador's Theatre); *I Am Telling You I'm Not Going* (Pleasance Theatre); *Tender Loving Care* (New Theatre Royal, Portsmouth); *The Witches of Eastwick* (Watermill Theatre); *Angus, Thongs and Even More Snogging* (West Yorkshire Playhouse) and *Schnapps* (Lyric Hammersmith). Her television credits include *Drifters*, and for film *At First Sight* and *Jitterman*.

George Taylor (ROB)

George Taylor's theatre credits include *Cleansed, A Woman Killed with Kindness* (National Theatre); *The Moderate Soprano, The Trial of Ubu* (Hampstead Theatre); *Death of a Salesman* (Royal & Derngate); *The Duchess of Malfi* (Oxford Playhouse); *The American Wife* (Park Theatre). Recent television includes *Wanderlust, Howards End, Loaded, Partners in Crime* and *Company X*. Recent film includes *The Lady in the Van, You and I, Sherlock Holmes: A Game of Shadows* and *Resistance*.

Frankie Bradshaw (Set and Costume Designer)

Frankie Bradshaw is an award-winning designer for theatre, dance and opera. She won the *Best Creative West End Debut* at the Stage Debut Awards 2019 jointly with director Lynette Linton for *Sweat* at the Gielgud Theatre and the *Off West-End Best Set Design* award in 2016. Theatre credits include: *Hamlet* (Dorfman/National Theatre tour); *Beautiful: The Carole King Musical* (Leicester Curve/UK tour). *Beauty and the Beast* (Rose Theatre, Kingston); *The Long Song* (Chichester Festival Theatre); *The Lemon Table* (MGC/Wiltshire Creative); *Piaf, Skellig* (Nottingham Playhouse); *Assembly* (Donmar Warehouse); *Sweat* (West End/Donmar Warehouse); *Two Trains Running* (ETT/Royal & Derngate); *Cinderella* (Lyric Hammersmith); *A Christmas Carol* (Theatre Clwyd); *Napoli Brooklyn* (UK tour/Park Theatre); *Trying It On* (UK tour/RSC/Royal Court); *Kiss Me Kate, Jerusalem, Nesting, Robin Hood* (Watermill Theatre); *Cookies* (Theatre Royal Haymarket); *On The Exhale* (Traverse); *Hansel* (Salisbury Playhouse). Opera designs include *Macbeth, Idomeneo* and *Elizabetta* (English Touring Opera); and for Dance, *Pinocchio* (Northern Ballet). www.frankiebradshawdesign.com

Bethany Gupwell (Lighting Designer)

Credits include: *Wolf Cub, Little Scratch* (Hampstead); *The Woods* (Southwark Playhouse); *Rice, Little Baby Jesus* (Orange Tree Theatre); *You Heard Me* (ARC Stockton and tour); *Interruptions* (Jackson's Lane

Theatre); *Albatross* (The Playground); *When Darkness Falls* (Park200); *Fitter, Wonder Winterland* (Soho Theatre); *Talking Heads* (Watford Palace); *Tipping the Velvet* (Mountview); *The Last Harvest* (National Youth Theatre); *Trade* (UK tour); *Queen of the Mist* (Charing Cross Theatre); *Keep Watching* (New Diorama); *Zorba* (Eve Lyons Theatre); *Chess* (Electric Theatre); *I'd Rather Go Blind* (Omnibus Theatre); *Dracula* (Leicester Curve); *Sweet Like Chocolate Boy* (Brockley Jack); *Madrigal, The Plaza, The Caucasian Chalk Circle, Free* (Royal Central School of Speech & Drama).

Megan Lucas (Video Designer)

Megan is a lighting and video designer, whose recent credits include: *The Wellspring* at Royal & Derngate, Northampton, as Video Designer; *Criptic Pit Party* at the Barbican, and *The Masks We Wear* at Royal & Derngate, both as Lighting Designer; and is an Associate Artist with Royal & Derngate. Originally training as both an architectural designer and graphic designer, she has worked across several theatrical productions, film, and music videos. She has a personal interest in accessible theatre and as a result she developed and programmed the hard-of-hearing captioning system currently in use at Royal & Derngate. She also collaborated with the same venue to create the NextGen: Lighting Design course, giving young people an introduction to the technical and creative skills involved in stage lighting design.

Jamie Lu (Sound Designer)

Jamie's previous work at the Arcola includes *Broken Lad* (2021). Theatre credits as sound designer include *Burnout* (SHYBAIRN Theatre); *The Slug Show* (Camden People's Theatre); *Tokyo Rose* (Southwark Playhouse/UK tour); *A Report to an Academy, Butterfly, The Most Beautiful Woman in the World* (Baron's Court Theatre); *Apollonia, Flowers for Algernon, Black Mary Poppins* (Focustage/Chinese tour); *Paper Crown* (Corbett Theatre/ Bloomsbury Festival); *Wild Duck* (West Side Theatre, ET Space, China); *The Sound of Music* (Chinese tour); *Sink* (Courtyard Theatre/Edinburgh Fringe/ Southbank Centre China Changing Festival); *String* (Lion and Unicorn Theatre). As Scenographer: *A Report to an Academy·Live, Choking Game* (Irrelevant Theatre). As Assistant Sound Designer: *Henry V* (Donmar Warehouse). Audio play: *The Dream Machine* (Fizzy Sherbet).

Olivia Ward (Costume Supervisor)

Olivia has worked in theatrical costume for the last ten years in running wardrobe on shows such as *Charlie and the Chocolate Factory, Dreamgirls, Old Times, The Audience*, and for many productions at the Almeida itself. As assistant supervisor: *Plenty* at Chichester Festival Theatre and *Hamlet* at the Young Vic. As supervisor: Young Company Season, Almeida Theatre 2019; *The Collaboration*, Young Vic Theatre 2022; *Daddy*, Almeida Theatre 2022.

Josephine Tremelling (Production Manager)

Josephine studied at Dartington College of arts obtaining a BA Hons in Contemporary Theatre before working as a drama facilitator and Co-Founding inclusive Theatre Company Anyone Everyone and Cabaret troupes The Thrill Billies and The Salacious Sirens. After deciding to broaden her technical theatre knowledge Josephine took the role of technician and later of Production Manager at the Pleasance Theatre and after this as a freelance PM and Lighting Designer. Her current projects include working with Ephemeral Ensemble, Theatre Re and The Little Angel Theatre.

Hayley Bowman (Stage Manager on Book)

Hayley's love of stage and theatre stemmed from attending dance school from the age of three. She regularly danced in shows and has performed at the Royal Albert Hall and Sadlers Wells. After gaining her A levels at a local performing arts school she secured a place on the Production and technical Theatre Arts course at the London Academy of Music and Dramatic Arts (LAMDA) specialising in Stage Management. Since qualifying in 2021 she has gone on to work as assistant stage manager on *Love and Other Acts of Violence* at the Donmar Warehouse, and on *The Chairs* at the Almeida Theatre

arcola
theatre

ARCOLA THEATRE was founded by Mehmet Ergen and Leyla Nazli in September 2000. Originally located in a former textile factory on Arcola Street in Dalston, in January 2011 the theatre moved to its current location in a former paint-manufacturing workshop on Ashwin Street. In 2021, we opened an additional outdoor performance space just round the corner from the main building: Arcola Outside.

Arcola Theatre produces daring, high-quality theatre in the heart of East London and beyond. We commission and premiere exciting, original works alongside rare gems of world drama and bold new productions of classics. Our socially engaged, international programme champions diversity, challenges the status quo, and attracts over 65,000 people to our building each year. Ticket prices are some of the most affordable in London. Every year, we offer 26 weeks of free rehearsal space to culturally diverse and refugee artists; our Grimeborn Festival opens up opera with contemporary stagings at affordable prices; and our Participation department creates over 13,500 creative opportunities for the people of Hackney and beyond. Our pioneering environmental initiatives are award-winning and aim to make Arcola the world's first carbon-neutral theatre. Arcola has won awards including the UK Theatre Award for Promotion of Diversity, The Stage Award for Sustainability and the Peter Brook Empty Space Award.

Twitter, Instagram and Facebook: @arcolatheatre
www.arcolatheatre.com   020 7503 1646

Executive

Artistic Director
Mehmet Ergen

Deputy Artistic Director &
Executive Producer
Leyla Nazli

General Management

General Manager
Lucy Wood

Fundraising and
Development Manager
Emma Attwell

Finance

Finance Manager
Steve Haygreen

Front of House

Front of House Supervisors
Lily Batikyan
Mary Roubos

Operations

Events and
Operations Manager
Nadja Bering Ovesen

Software Developer
and IT Support
Oliver Brill

Facilities Maintenance
Niall Bateson

Participation

Participation Manager
Charlotte Croft

Production

Chief Technician
Michael Paget

Cleaning

Cleaners
Mary Rodriguez
Marisol Rojas

Trustees

Ben Todd (Chair)
Gabriel Gbadamosi
Lynne McKenzie
Jack Shepherd
Abdullah Tercanli

We Started to Sing

Barney Norris is a playwright and novelist. His work has received awards from the International Theatre Institute, the Critics' Circle, the *Evening Standard*, the Society of Authors and the South Bank Sky Arts Times Breakthrough Awards, among others, and been translated into eight languages. His plays include *Visitors*, *Nightfall* and an acclaimed adaptation of Kazuo Ishiguro's *The Remains of the Day*; his novels include *Five Rivers Met on a Wooded Plain*.

by the same author

THE WELLSPRING
with David Owen Norris

BARNEY NORRIS

We Started to Sing

faber

First published in 2022
by Faber and Faber Limited
74–77 Great Russell Street
London WC1B 3DA

Typeset by Brighton Gray
Printed and bound in the UK by CPI Group (Ltd), Croydon CR0 4YY

All rights reserved
© Barney Norris, 2022

Barney Norris is hereby identified as author
of this work in accordance with Section 77 of the
Copyright, Designs and Patents Act 1988

All rights whatsoever in this work, amateur or professional,
are strictly reserved. Applications for permission for any use
whatsoever including performance rights must be made in
advance, prior to any such proposed use, to Dalzell & Beresford Ltd,
Paddock Suite, The Courtyard, 55 Charterhouse Street, London EC1M 6HA

No performance may be given unless a licence
has first been obtained

This book is sold subject to the condition that it shall not,
by way of trade or otherwise, be lent, resold, hired out
or otherwise circulated without the publisher's prior consent
in any form of binding or cover other than that in which
it is published and without a similar condition including
this condition being imposed on the subsequent purchaser

A CIP record for this book
is available from the British Library

978-0-571-37799-2

2 4 6 8 10 9 7 5 3 1

Author's Note

Between 2016 and 2020, several difficult things happened to me, just as my life as a storyteller was supposedly beginning. It is not an exaggeration to say that, as a result, there were times when I did not know who I was any more.

One day I had the idea of working out this problem by writing down my own story, and piecing together the things which made up 'me'.

The result is a study of the people whose lives led to mine. I share it with a kind of defiance, as a way of insisting that, *yes*, life is worthwhile as I have experienced it thus far, because love like this can be found in the course of it. I am proud to be able to answer in the affirmative, having tested the matter to something approaching destruction.

Perhaps I ought to say for legal reasons that any resemblances to real persons, living or dead, are purely coincidental; but that would be dishonest. These are my parents and grandparents. My rendering of them may well vary wildly from who they really are, or were, because this is a play about memory, not reality. I was only present at three of these scenes, and some of the others never exactly happened – they're true stories in a slightly different way. But to me they're still true stories.

My brother and I stopped talking for several years because we disagreed over the ethics of telling. When my father remarried a few years ago, he chose for a reading 'There is no remembrance of former things'. Still, here I am, a former thing remembering, because even if some of my family wish I wouldn't, it's the only way I know to say I love them, and that I am grateful to them for having brought me to this place, and for having kept the sparrow in the feasting hall over the course of the last few years.

5

I'd like to thank Leyla, Mehmet, Emma, Jack, Michael, Lucy and everyone at Arcola Theatre; Dinah, Jodi and all at Faber and Faber; Rachel, Iain and everyone at the Lyric Hammersmith; Helen Baxendale, Simon Beresford, Hayley Bowman, Frankie Bradshaw, Susan Brown, Jude Christian, Emily Compton, Hasan Dixon, Anthony O'Donnell, Timmy Fisher, Kara Fitzpatrick, Barbara Flynn, Ian Gelder, Bethany Gupwell, Beth Lawson, Jamie Lu, Megan Lucas, Lily Nichol, Naomi Petersen, Rebecca Pitt, David Ricardo-Pearce, Kirris Riviere, Robin Soans, George Taylor, Josephine Tremelling, Sam Troughton, Sue Wallace, Liv Ward, Josh Zaré; and my family, pictured herein.

Barney Norris
April 2022

i.m. Iris Bellis
My grandmother
Who died the night before we started rehearsals

We Started to Sing was first performed at Arcola Theatre, London, on 19 May 2022, with the following cast:

David David Ricardo-Pearce
Peggy Barbara Flynn
Bert Robin Soans
Fiona Naomi Petersen
Rob George Taylor

Director Barney Norris
Set and Costume Designer Frankie Bradshaw
Lighting Designer Bethany Gupwell
Musical Arranger Timmy Fisher
Sound Designer Jamie Lu
Costume Supervisor Olivia Ward
Production Manager Josephine Tremelling
Stage Manager on Book Hayley Bowman
Assistant Stage Manager Emily Compton
ASM Student Placement Elsie O'Rourke
Dialect Consultant Mary Howland

Characters

David
Peggy
Bert
Fiona
Rob

WE STARTED TO SING

'Down their carved names the rain-drop ploughs.'
Thomas Hardy, 'During Wind and Rain'

Note

This story spans three decades, and the characters age significantly. They should nonetheless be played by the same actor in each scene.

Act One

A piano and chairs. Projections across the space.

David sits down at the piano. He plays the initial piano sketch for Elgar's Cello Concerto. Then the lights go down, and . . .

The light of evening. There is a bottle of wine and four glasses. Peggy is seated. Bert is coming back in from the loo. David stands with his arm up behind his back as if he's in a half-nelson. Then sits down as Bert comes in.

Bert They'll be out like lights.

David Let's hope so.

Bert Up late.

David To celebrate you, Bert.

Peggy And isn't that lovely.

David And they did go to bed on time, it's just they woke up.

Bert has sat down.

Bert They'll be back off soon enough.

Peggy Wasn't it a lovely dinner?

Bert Oh, yes. Fantastic day, Dave.

David I'm glad you enjoyed it.

Bert Oh yeah. Your boys.

Peggy They're great, aren't they.

David They are.

Peggy Enjoying themselves.

Bert Makes you feel young again.

Peggy laughs.

Peggy If only.

Bert On your seventieth.

Peggy *Your* seventieth, I'm only sixty-eight.

Bert And it's not actually my birthday, either.

David All right, Dad.

Bert Close enough. And those two are –

David Yeah.

Peggy What did they call that tree they liked on the walk, the dancing tree?

Beat. Bert gets up, speaking without moving away from the chair again. He stands with his arm up behind his back as if he's in a half-nelson.

Bert They'll be out like lights.

David Let's hope so.

Bert Up late.

David To celebrate you, Bert.

Peggy And isn't that lovely.

David And they did go to bed on time, it's just they woke up.

Bert sits down.

Bert They'll be back off soon enough.

Peggy Wasn't it a lovely dinner?

Bert Oh, yes. Fantastic day, Dave.

David I'm glad you enjoyed it.

Bert Oh yeah. Your boys.

Peggy They're great, aren't they.

David They are.

Peggy Enjoying themselves.

Bert Makes you feel young again.

Peggy laughs.

Peggy If only.

Bert On your seventieth.

Peggy *Your* seventieth, I'm only sixty-eight.

Bert And it's not actually my birthday, either.

David All right, Dad.

Bert Close enough. And those two are –

David Yeah.

Peggy They liked that tree on the walk, the dancing tree.

Bert German.

David Tanzlinden. I think Iris named it. Or Fiona named it while her mum was here. But that's what they call it anyway.

Bert Tanzlinden means dancing tree.

David Big thing over there. Bit like the maypole. And some places they climb up in them, platforms and rooms, like The Faraway Tree.

Peggy Spoonface.

Bert I don't know much about Germany.

Peggy You know about Leipzig.

David Oh, Leipzig.

Bert That was beautiful, wasn't it. Only place we didn't bomb flat, that's why. Only place they didn't have to start all over again.

Peggy You've been back since, haven't you.

David A few times, for concerts.

Peggy I loved that holiday very much.

Bert I got some good film on the camera today.

David Yes?

Bert I'll have to bring it next time we come down and we can have a look.

David Great.

Bert Or we'll watch it next time you come home.

Enter Fiona. Peggy stands. She stands with her arm up behind her back as if she's in a half-nelson.

Fiona They're down!

Peggy Oh, well done.

David Well done, love. Drink?

Fiona sits.

Fiona Thank you.

Bert I got some good film on the camera today.

David Yes?

Bert I'll have to bring it next time we come down and we can have a look.

David Great.

Bert Or we'll watch it next time you come home.

Fiona They're down!

Peggy Oh, well done.

David Well done, love. Drink?

Fiona Thank you.

18

Bert Here you go, mate.

Bert pushes the wine bottle over to David.

David Thanks, Bert.

David stands and circles the table with the wine, refills Fiona's glass first, then tops up Peggy and Bert's.

Peggy What did you read them?

Fiona *Hand, Hand, Fingers, Thumb.*

Peggy Oh, yes.

Bert I never heard that, I don't think.

Peggy Good one.

Fiona Dr Seuss.

Peggy recites a line from the book.

David *Cat in the Hat.*

Bert I know that one.

David Famous one, that.

Peggy recites another line from the book, then she and Fiona recite a line together.

Bert Cheers.

Fiona clinks glasses with Bert. Bert has a drink. David sits.

That's lovely, that.

Peggy You'll have a sore head tomorrow.

Bert Probably will.

Fiona I didn't think you drank.

Bert I don't much.

Peggy But special occasions.

David Which is what this is.

Bert Well.

Peggy Bert.

Fiona We are sorry we weren't there on the day.

Peggy Oh –

Fiona Just the boys, and the move, you know.

Peggy We know what it's like, we had boys too, remember.

Bert And how could you have known when my birthday was? Tell you what I ought to do, I should have it the same day every year, then it'd be easier to keep track of.

Fiona Oh, Bert.

Bert Only joking.

David We didn't know you were having a party.

Bert I'm joking. Just a funny day to book the moving van, that's all.

David We didn't know about the party.

Bert We'd have helped. Helped you move.

David We didn't want to impose.

Bert Certainly didn't do that.

Peggy You shut up, Bert Norris, stop trying to start a fight.

Bert Oh, sorry. Only a joke. Sorry, Fiona. Dave.

Fiona No, we're sorry.

Peggy All right then.

Bert Call us next time you want any help though.

David We didn't know you were having a party.

Bert I'm joking. Just a funny day to book the moving van, that's all.

David We didn't know about the party.

Bert We'd have helped. Helped you move.

David We didn't want to impose.

Bert Certainly didn't do that.

Peggy You shut up, Bert Norris, and stop trying to start a fight.

Bert Oh, sorry. Only a joke. Sorry, Fiona. Dave.

Fiona No, we're sorry.

Peggy All right then.

Bert Call us next time you want any help though.

Peggy Barnaby's very good at his reading now, isn't he?

Fiona Oh, yeah.

Bert A prodigy!

Peggy He is a prodigy.

David Well.

Fiona There are kids in his class can't read at all yet.

Peggy You're putting the work in. Josiah will be the same.

Fiona Hopefully.

David Not that we're measuring them against each other.

Peggy No, of course. I just mean you're doing it all so well.

Fiona Thank you.

Fiona stands with her arm up behind her back as if she's in a half-nelson.

Bert We had less than this to drink on our wedding day.

David gets up, clears away the high chair.

Peggy That's true.

Fiona Really?

David One bottle of sherry on your wedding day.

Bert Between thirteen.

Fiona Really?

Peggy The middle of the war. We've told you this story.

Fiona I don't know.

David You probably have.

Fiona I don't think you have.

David Walked into that one.

Bert We were married while I was on leave. That's why it was Christmas Day, I had shore leave for Christmas and never another bloody day in the year. So I wrote ahead to say I was coming, and how about tying the knot and that, and on Christmas Eve I got the train up to Long Buckby Wharf, and walked the last six miles to my dad's house, and for dinner I had the rice pudding he'd left out for the dogs. Next morning we were married in the Baptist chapel, and for the breakfast there was a bottle of sherry.

Peggy Between thirteen.

David Some people wouldn't have sat down at that table.

Peggy Unlucky number.

Bert Then the next morning we heard everyone was getting an extra day's leave, but had to report to the train station so it'd be known we hadn't buggered off. And Peggy said she'd come along with me to check in.

Peggy I did.

Bert I had a friend was a taxi driver, and he gave us a lift, except his petrol ration ran out on the way, so we had to walk the last couple of miles.

David And when you got there –

Bert And when we got there, the bloke told me it was only army had an extra day, and I had to get on the train and go back for that evening! So I gave her a kiss on the platform, didn't I, and it was three years before we saw one another again.

Peggy There's a way to start a marriage.

Bert Peace and quiet.

Peggy Quite.

Fiona Three years?

David sits down again.

Peggy That's right. Even when we did meet next, it was only chance. I was working in London. Secretarial work. And I'd bought this carpet, for my digs. I was living on Frognal, up in Finchley, see, and a bomb had come down over the road and we'd lost all the glass from our windows, and I was working to make it nice again. So I'd got this carpet and I had it on my shoulder, but it was too heavy for me, a great big thing. And I was struggling along the platform at Waterloo station when I heard this voice saying, 'Can I help you with that?' And that was Bert.

Fiona No.

Bert I'd just got back in the country.

Fiona Question is, Bert, did you know it was Peggy or did you used to say that to all the pretty girls?

Bert Oh, you know me.

Peggy Yes, we do.

Bert It seems unbelievable doesn't it, but these things did happen. In the war they happened a lot, I used to think. I met your brother on a beach in Malaysia.

Peggy You did.

Bert Saw this ship coming into port and thought to myself I know that ship, I think Ted might be on that. And sure enough, I found him on the beach an hour later. Other side of the bloody world. And there's my brother Harold, in the first war, my half-brother.

Fiona Oh?

Bert Harold was travelling by train to the south coast for deployment, after training. And on the way down he passed through Buckby. And he wrote a postcard to his parents, my dad and his first wife, and he threw it out the train window as the train went through. And do you know, someone found it, and brought it to my father? And it was the last thing they ever heard from him, he died of wounds in France.

Fiona How sad.

Bert These things somehow happen in a war. I was on shore leave from the *Hood* when the *Hood* was sunk, and that was a kind of miracle as well. There were only three survivors from the *Hood*. Those who were actually on the ship, I mean.

Peggy I was with him that day.

Fiona Were you?

Peggy We were in a hotel by the sea up in the north-east, was it Hull, was it . . . Whitby? I'd travelled up to see him while he had leave.

Bert I don't remember where it was.

Peggy We went for a walk after breakfast, and Bert wore his uniform, and his cap said HMS *Hood*, you know. And a man came up to us and said excuse me, are you on the *Hood*? And Bert said yes, and he said your ship's sunk, mate. We hardly believed him.

Bert A lot of the ships I served on sunk. We were holed in Scapa Flow, we were bombed in Narvik. I won the Croix de Guerre for Narvik. I was with the Free French by that time. I'd volunteered for submarine duty, I was tired of the ships I was on getting sunk.

Peggy Even though submarines were more dangerous really.

Bert But you get sent to whatever special duties they need men for, so I ended up in the French Resistance.

David stands.

David I'll just go to the loo.

Fiona Okay.

David exits.

Peggy You've upset him.

Bert It was meant to be a joke, we don't mind really.

Fiona We are sorry.

Peggy It's nicer to be able to do it like this. All those candles you put on the cake!

Bert We blaze brighter as we go on!

Peggy Apologise to him properly when he comes back.

Bert I'd only rake it up again, he's fine.

Fiona I'm sure he's fine. He's just embarrassed.

Bert I think so. Just tired. Busy day today.

Peggy Too much to drink.

Bert Well yes.

Peggy We should go to bed really.

Fiona It's all right.

Bert We probably should though.

Fiona Are you all right about the caravan? I'm worried about you out there.

Peggy Oh, we love it. Nicer than indoors.

Bert Holidays were always caravans for us. Makes us feel at home. Take the caravan to Devon or to Wales on the back of the car, strap the boats to it, get the boys in the water.

Fiona Did you have boats?

Peggy Bert made kayaks.

Fiona You made them?

Bert My woodworking.

Fiona Boats!

Bert They're quite simple really.

Fiona I suppose it seems impressive because they have to float.

Bert I'll have to make some for your boys.

Fiona Would you?

Bert Course. Dave's not going to, is he. Not so good with his hands.

Peggy Well he is good with his hands, he's a professional concert pianist.

Bert Yeah. He is good. Just a different kind of – you know.

Enter David. He doesn't sit down.

David Hello.

Bert I was just going to tell your good lady about my adventure in the Congo!

David Oh yeah?

Fiona The Congo?

26

David Bert got shipwrecked. It might not have been the Congo.

Bert Africa, anyway.

Fiona You were shipwrecked?

Bert Ran aground, yeah. And the ship went down. Had to swim to shore.

Peggy This tribal village took him in.

Fiona Really?

Bert Me and a dozen others who survived. Like something out of a book. The women had no tops on.

Peggy Bert.

Bert We slept in these huts with fires in the middle. But then after a week or so I got the impression the tribal elders were trying to marry me off to one of the local girls, and I was already married of course, I didn't much like that. So I swapped my leather jacket for a coracle with this bloke I'd got friendly with, and me and my mate went to the coast and waited till we saw a ship passing, and we paddled out to it and got a lift home. A lot of the crew of that ship drowned.

Fiona You've seen such a lot.

Bert Well, that's war, isn't it. I'd never have gone anywhere if it wasn't for the war.

Peggy My dad moved around.

Bert He did.

Peggy That wasn't war.

Fiona What happened to him, Peggy?

David reaches for the wine.

David Shall we finish this off?

Peggy Oh, thank you.

David There you go.

David pours out the last of the bottle.

Bert Just a bit for me.

Fiona You were saying about your dad.

David stays standing.

Peggy Oh yes, that was poverty got him moving. He was a farmer in North Wales, in Ffestiniog. Grey place. Quite beautiful. And the Forestry Commission bought him out. Not that he minded much. He used to say he starved in winter.

David Ended up as groundsman at Daventry golf course.

Peggy In the end. After he'd been a driver in all sorts of places, a London bus, a taxi in Rochester, he drove an officer round in Persia in the First World War. When he came to Northamptonshire he used to drive the farmer round in his two Daimlers, and the farmer let him use them if he went away. Then he set up on his own on Borough Hill. We lived in a cottage at the top of the course and farmed the hill beneath the telegraph masts, we kept sheep. Big stone bowl in the cellar for butter churning, mice would fall in. I used to walk to school over the course, because we looked after that as well as farming the other side of the hill, see, and my job was to take a stick with me, long flat stick, and knock the worms, casts off the greens.

Bert Our world was a lovely place to be young.

Peggy It was still a bit like that for you I think, when you were growing up.

David The land that time forgot.

Peggy Yes.

David All the women still covered their heads. Headscarves, I mean.

Peggy We did, yes.

David A different world.

Bert I miss it.

Peggy Of course you do, Bert. That's what it's like having been young.

Bert I miss it.

Fiona My grandfather was a driver.

Peggy Was he?

Fiona He drove ambulances in the war.

Bert Dangerous work.

Peggy Was he a driver in civilian life as well?

Fiona Oh, he had a thousand jobs. He worked on the docks at Poplar, he was in service. And he was an ambulance driver again for a time. Had to go to the Farnborough air crash.

Bert No.

Fiona Terrible.

Bert I was at the Farnborough air crash.

Fiona You weren't.

Bert For work. I was running a stall there. We might have met, me and him.

Fiona That's amazing. I mean it must have been terrible to see.

Bert Worse for your grandfather, pulling them out.

Peggy That was your mother's father, was it?

Fiona That's it.

Peggy How is Iris, is she all right?

Fiona Oh, she's fine, thanks.

Peggy And your dad?

Fiona Yes, fine. We haven't seen them recently, but they're doing all right, I think.

Peggy Hard when you don't all live nearby.

Fiona It is.

Bert And when you're so busy moving on people's birthdays.

Peggy Bert.

Bert Joking!

Peggy Honestly. (*She claps her hands together.*) We ought to go to bed.

Peggy gets up. Fiona gets up after her.

David Yes, I'm tired.

Bert Busy day, wasn't it.

David Are you off in the morning?

Fiona Oh.

David I just mean you'll want to get back.

Peggy Yes, we'll leave in the morning. Breakfast first then off, if that's all right.

Bert gets up.

Fiona Of course. It's been so lovely to have you here.

Peggy It's lovely to see your new home.

Fiona I like this part of the country. We were looking at Wales before we went for here, but I think this is better.

Peggy Were you looking at Wales?

Fiona Round Hay-on-Wye, you know?

Peggy Oh, of course.

Bert Used to go on holidays.

Fiona Did you?

David I told you that, didn't I?

Fiona Maybe you did. We were looking in Kington.

David Thought of opening a music school. The Tonypandy music school. There in the Beacons, on the mountainside.

Fiona But then the organist job came up, and it came with the cottage, and it's closer to London, it just made more sense.

Bert Long way from anywhere, Hay-on-Wye.

Fiona Exactly. So we thought we'd come here, and now we're in this place I think it's perfect.

Bert It's a lovely arrangement.

David Yes.

Peggy yawns.

Bert Keeping you up?

Peggy Oh, sorry.

David Set us all off.

Peggy We must get to bed, I think.

Bert Yes, come on.

Peggy Too long nattering! We don't always drink this much.

Fiona Such a wonderful evening. The boys loved seeing you.

Peggy turns to leave.

Peggy And we loved seeing them. Come on, Bert. Night, Fiona.

Fiona Goodnight, Peggy.

Peggy Dave.

David Goodnight, Mum.

Bert turns to leave.

Fiona You're sure you're all right outside?

David Oh, they love it. See you in the morning!

Peggy That we will.

Bert Come on, Peggy. Night, both.

Fiona Night night.

David I'll see you out.

David follows them.

Peggy Oh, thanks.

David Come on then.

David, Peggy and Bert exit. Fiona picks up a glass. Very slowly, she holds the glass up to the light, looks through it. Then, at normal pace, she collects up more glasses to take to the kitchen. David comes back in.

Fiona They're great.

David Yeah.

Fiona exits. David collects up glasses. Fiona enters.

Fiona We should have gone to his birthday.

David He'll be all right. We weren't free.

David exits with the glasses to the kitchen.

Fiona We shouldn't have said the movers came that day, he knows we're fibbing.

David (*off*) We were busy though. It can't always be about Bert.

Fiona Okay.

David enters.

David Well, you know what I mean.

David sits back down at the table with Fiona.

He liked getting out all his stories for you.

Fiona He doesn't know what I've heard and what I haven't.

David Runs on train tracks, can't be diverted.

Fiona But that's how you do it, that's what a family is.

David What?

Fiona Telling stories. We'll go to your mum's birthday.

David Yeah.

Fiona You know they are wonderful people, don't you.

David It's just the tall tree thing.

Fiona They're very proud of you.

David It's just an environment I left, and it's strange to enter back into it like that. Shall we clean that lot up in the morning?

Fiona God yes.

Fiona stands and stretches. She thinks for a moment.

I wish there could be a day where families came together and just said it all to each other.

David All what?

Fiona Everything they felt.

David That would be disastrous.

Fiona No. Just say it all out. Because then everyone would know it all, and there'd be nothing left to hurt anyone.

David You think that would bring people closer?

Fiona There'd be nothing in the way any more of saying we love each other. What are you thinking?

David Sorry?

Fiona You're quiet.

David Oh. When they left the room just now, and I came back in and you were here, I had the strangest feeling that none of it had happened. And they were just a dream. I was just thinking of that.

> 'I have been here before,
> But when or how I cannot tell;
> I know the grass beyond the door,
> The sweet keen smell,
> The sighing sound, the lights around the shore.'

Fiona They're all right out there?

David In the caravan? They love it.

A baby cries.

Josiah.

Fiona Here we go.

David stands.

David My turn tonight.

Fiona You sure?

David Absolutely. You sleep.

Fiona Thanks.

David Lovely evening.

Fiona It was.

David Love you.

Fiona Yeah. Love you too.

Lights change. David sits at the piano, and Fiona is standing alone.

2

Fiona and David perform Purcell's 'When I Am Laid in Earth'. Peggy and Bert enter. Then Fiona and David stop playing, and we see . . .

Peggy, Bert and Fiona are onstage, putting up shelves. The only new prop is a cardboard box containing some toys. Fiona removes her arm from under someone's head in a bed – while still standing, it's just the mnemonic marking gesture – and the scene begins.

Bert Could you pass me that, Peggy?

Peggy Here you go.

Peggy passes Bert a drill.

Bert Thank you.

Bert starts putting up shelves.

Fiona This is looking great, Bert.

Bert Should be all right.

Fiona I'm so grateful to you.

Peggy We're glad to be of use. We'll always be here to help if you need us.

Bert We could put this on now.

Fiona Oh, great.

Bert Just a bit – this way.

Peggy That's good.

Bert You all right, Peg?

Peggy I'm fine.

Bert You've done your end, Fiona.

Fiona Okay.

Bert It's a nice place, this. You'll be all right here.

Fiona I hope so.

Bert You've chosen very well. Are the schools good?

Fiona There's one the other side of Putney high street they'll go to. Seems nice.

Bert They can walk to school can they, they don't have to catch a bus?

Fiona Yes, I'll walk them there I think.

Bert That's good.

Peggy As long as it doesn't interfere with your being able to work.

Bert I'll get the screws in now, and we'll be done.

Fiona Thank you so much.

Peggy It's going to be a very different life. Big change from where you were.

Bert Here we go.

Peggy I always thought it might be too far out of things, before. For young people.

Fiona Well, they did love it. It just wasn't practical any more.

Peggy I meant you. A young woman needs some life around her. This will be a better place for you.

Fiona I wish it could have worked out. Me and David. I hope you know that.

Peggy I know. But things happen. And we'll always be here to support you and the boys.

Fiona And David's all right.

Peggy He's holding up.

Fiona I know not being with the boys –

Peggy Yes.

Fiona I'm never going to keep him away from them though.

Peggy Of course you won't.

Fiona He's still in America I think.

Peggy All those concerts.

Fiona It's great.

Peggy They just rang him up out the blue, you know.

Fiona Yes, I know.

Peggy Of course you do, I'm sorry.

Fiona And he went.

Peggy And he went.

Fiona And never came back.

Peggy Well.

Fiona That's unfair, I'm sorry.

Peggy If that's how you feel. How are Barnaby and Josiah coping with it all?

Fiona Oh, all right I think. They don't really understand, of course. I don't think they really wanted to leave where we were.

Peggy And you two are getting on all right when you have to see each other?

37

Fiona I hope so. We weren't. But I was talking to my lawyer and she said to me, you have children together. You're going to have a relationship with this man for the rest of your life. So I tried to snap out of it.

Peggy It had grown fractious.

Fiona I don't want it to be.

Bert That's all done now.

Fiona Oh, thank you so much.

Bert Looks pretty good.

Fiona It does. You are clever, Bert.

Bert I've always thought so.

Peggy And how are things with you and your mum?

Fiona Oh, not so good I'm afraid.

Peggy Oh dear.

Fiona That's been very difficult, on top of – (*She cries.*) I'm sorry.

Peggy Oh, Fiona.

Peggy comforts Fiona. Bert clocks what's going on and decides to get out of there.

Bert Shall I pack up my tools downstairs?

Peggy Why don't you?

Bert Course.

Fiona I'm sorry.

Bert One minute. You two –

Bert exits, taking his toolkit with him.

Fiona I'm sorry.

Peggy Don't apologise, love.

Fiona I'm all right.

Peggy Of course you are.

Fiona It's just my dad.

Peggy It's very hard you've had to deal with both things at once.

Fiona I sent him a letter the day before he died to tell him it was over between me and David. And then the next day, it was my birthday, and the phone rang, and it was Mum saying he'd gone. I got in the car and drove straight there, and Mum came out of the house and the first thing she said was he didn't read the letter. He was in the car. I don't know where they were going. Now we've stopped talking.

Peggy You and your mum?

Fiona Not since the funeral.

Peggy Why?

Fiona Everything's different now, you know? I don't think we know how to do it any more.

Peggy It's a difficult situation.

Fiona I don't really know what I'm going to do.

Peggy Do you think it would ever be possible to sit down with her like we are now?

Fiona I don't know whether I could. They'd call it post-natal depression now. The way she was after she had her children. My brother remembers it, he's the eldest. I should be sympathetic, I suppose.

Peggy Yes.

Fiona There's a cage around her. Mum was a child in the Blitz. She's younger than you. And when she was six she caught diphtheria, and had to be in this hospital, on a high floor, she had a view of the fires and the bombs coming down. They kept her in a sort of cage for six weeks, with another little boy who had it too, and at weekends her parents would come and see her through the bars, but they couldn't touch her. When they let her home they burned everything she'd taken in. And she'd taken her favourite bear, no one told her what was going to happen. I sometimes think she's still in there. If something like that happens to you, you never get out of it. You get left behind with the bear.

Enter Bert.

Bert You two all right?

Peggy We're fine. We were just talking about Fiona's dad.

Bert Oh, yes. We were so sorry about Alan.

Fiona Thank you.

Bert He was a lovely man. I remember him at Josiah's christening, he wouldn't let go of that boy. Held him all afternoon. I've got it on video.

Fiona He did, didn't he.

Bert And Josiah happy sleeping on his shoulder.

Peggy We don't want to upset Fiona, Bert.

Bert I'm sorry.

Fiona No, it's nice you remember him like that. It's good. I worry Josiah won't remember him at all.

Bert Too young you mean.

Fiona Barnaby might. Six is old enough to remember things.

Peggy Yes, I'm sure.

Bert He liked to do funny voices.

Fiona Yes. Did he do them with you?

Bert Funny accents, quite a talent I thought.

Offstage, the doorbell rings. Bert removes his arm from under someone's head.

Fiona Oh.

Peggy Is that your door?

Fiona I think it is, yeah. I think it might be my friend Rob.

Peggy Oh right?

Fiona He said he'd come and help me unpack boxes.

Peggy Best to let him in then.

Fiona Yes. Okay, yeah. Let me go and see if it's him.

Fiona exits.

Bert Rob.

Peggy Her friend who's going to help her with unpacking.

Bert Mm-hm.

Peggy Well even if it is, they've been separated six months, it's not exactly scandalous.

Bert Mm-hm. Goody.

Peggy What do you mean, goody?

Bert There is a certain – exquisite pleasure to be taken in moments such as this one at how deeply awkward you are making everyone else feel simply by your presence.

Peggy Not everyone takes pleasure in that.

Bert No, but I find it very funny.

Enter Fiona and Rob.

Fiona Peggy, Bert. This is my friend Rob.

Rob Hello.

Bert Hello, Rob.

Beat.

Fiona Peggy, Bert. This is my friend Rob.

Rob Hello.

Bert Hello, Rob.

Peggy Nice to meet you.

Fiona Rob's a singer, we're doing a lot of gigs for the Sixteen together.

Peggy Oh yes. We like the Sixteen.

Rob I thought you'd probably want some help moving in. Didn't realise there'd already be people on hand, I'm sorry.

Peggy I think that's very helpful of you to have come.

Rob Well I know you've got the boys back tomorrow.

Bert Have you met our grandsons?

Rob Yes. Just the once. Great kids.

Peggy Aren't they.

Fiona You lot don't have to live with them. Joking.

Rob We know.

Fiona I mean they're fine to live with, apart from being – kids.

Bert Yeah.

Peggy So how long have you been in the Sixteen, Rob?

Rob Oh, a little while now. Coming up ten years.

Peggy You must enjoy it then.

Rob It's great. And the job I had before was working nights on a petrol station forecourt, so it's definitely better than that.

Bert Did you really?

Rob In Norwich, yeah.

Bert Good for you.

Peggy Are you doing any concerts at the moment, then?

Rob Bits and bobs. I sing at the Drome as well, for the services, so I'm always doing something.

Peggy What's the Drome?

Rob Oh, sorry. Westminster Cathedral. The Westminster Hippodrome, they call it.

Peggy Oh. Right.

Rob Sort of – singer's joke.

Bert Was it a Shell where you worked then, or an Esso, what was it?

Rob God, I can hardly remember. Wiped it from my mind. Shell I think.

Bert I like a Shell.

Peggy Bert.

Rob Good sausage rolls.

Bert Yes. Tell you what, I noticed the time while I was packing up downstairs, Peg, we ought to be going I reckon.

Peggy Why don't we . . .?

Fiona Of course, I'm sorry.

Bert Is there anything else you want us to do?

Fiona No, thank you, you've done so much.

Peggy We're glad to.

Bert I hope those shelves are all right. Crumbly plaster. I tidied up. But if it goes again. You just say if there are problems and we'll get it sorted out.

Fiona Thank you.

Peggy You'll be all right tonight?

Fiona I will.

Peggy We'd best make a start then.

Fiona Are you sure? You could stay if you liked. There are bunkbeds, after all.

Peggy Oh, no, it's an easy journey. Up the M1.

Bert We like the M1.

Peggy We got to go on the M1 before it opened. I taught one of the boys in school who was putting out the cones at Watford Gap. He let us do a mile of it for fun. There's a claim to fame for you.

Fiona It is.

Bert Got to go on Silverstone before it opened too. Same thing, knew a feller ran the hot dog stall and he let us in.

Peggy All right, Bert, that's enough claims to fame for tonight.

Bert You'll call us tomorrow if anything goes wrong?

Fiona I will. Are you all right with that?

Bert Perfectly thank you. Goodnight then.

Fiona Safe journey.

Bert You can always call us.

Fiona Thank you.

Peggy Goodnight, Fiona. Very nice to meet you, Rob.

Rob Lovely to meet you too. Safe journey.

Bert Thanks so much.

Fiona I'll show you out.

Peggy, Bert and Fiona exit. Fiona comes back in. They laugh.

I didn't think you were coming. I've got quite a lot done.

Rob Must be something I can help with?

Fiona Have a drink with me.

Rob I can help with that.

Fiona I need to put that lot away as well before I go to bed.

Rob What is it?

Fiona Their clothes, their things. The rest of the house can be a bomb site but I want them to recognise their room.

Rob All right. You get the wine, I'll make a start.

Fiona You sure?

Rob Absolutely. I'm doing toys though, toys are more fun.

Fiona One second.

Fiona exits. Rob opens a box of children's toys and starts going through them. Fiona enters with wine and glasses.

Rob I love these Transformer things.

Fiona Oh. Yeah, they're fun.

Rob Do they like them more as cars or spacemen?

Fiona Dinosaurs. They have dinosaur ones they like best.

Rob Fair enough.

Fiona Here you go.

Rob Thank you. This is Snoopy.

Fiona Your powers of observation are second to none.

Rob Well it is!

Fiona Yeah. Barnaby likes him. I want to get rid of some of his bears, he's got hundreds of bears.

Rob That bunkbed's bright orange.

Fiona Oh, yeah. Bert made them. He got a job lot of very cheap, very orange wood years ago and he's still working through it. Everything he makes is orange.

Rob Fair enough.

Fiona He talks about it like it's normal, is it normal being able to just make things? He's made a guitar and a harpsichord and a grandfather clock, I can't believe the country's just full of people who know how to do that.

Rob I think you'd be surprised.

Fiona It's inspiring. Or frightening.

Rob Why frightening?

Fiona That people can do these things and no one might know.

Rob They might not want the attention.

Fiona Surely everyone does?

Rob I think people like you and me, performers, we have a bit missing. That means we want to be looked at and applauded. I think it's almost an illness, wanting to be on a stage. In the paper.

Fiona So what's missing?

Rob I don't know. Probably different every time.

Fiona But you and me, what are we missing? I was so sad the whole time they were here. Because they did become like parents to me, they were like a new mum and dad. And now it's ending, we were doing all this and I think we all knew it was the last time we'd work together. Even if we keep in touch, we're never going to be really together again. And I wish I could have had that with my mum.

Rob Is that what's missing?

Fiona No, not that.

Rob But you're not close.

Fiona I used to think I knew what it was going to be like. They were my family, and I was married, I had the boys, I was going to sing. Now there's just the boys. I can't even sing now. Too scared. I got rid of my agent.

Rob So what's missing?

Fiona My dad died.

A breath.

Rob I don't talk to my mum either.

Fiona Really?

Rob After my dad died. Snap.

Fiona How come?

Rob It became impossible. I was – I found my twenties hard. I was in a bad relationship, and things got worse and worse, so one day I got up and left. Packed a bag and lived – out of the world for three years, more or less. Used to sleep in a tent. Less in the third year, I didn't bother putting it up in the third year so much unless it was raining. I travelled round. Got jobs sometimes, or sometimes I wouldn't have one. I was a welder's mate in Amsterdam. Then after three years the money ran out. And I'd been to pretty much every town in England, and my favourite was Norwich. So I got a train there, got a job on a forecourt, and started again. By then it was more or less done with my mum. Tried a few times, but it was done.

Fiona What's that like?

Rob What?

Fiona Being Laurie Lee.

Rob It scares me.

Fiona Why?

Rob Once you know it can happen, then you know it could happen again. None of the world might be real and for ever. Everything might just be for now. So you're not going to sing any more?

Fiona I don't know. When I'm singing, it's the least imperfect I ever feel. I'm above my life, looking down. But it always ends. I come back into my body. What?

Rob What happened next?

Lights change. Peggy and Bert are onstage; they start to sing.

3

Peggy and Bert sing the beginning of Sullivan's 'The Long Day Closes'. At the end of their song, they take their seats and watch the scene.

Rob and David enter. Both men rub their right hand deliberately, slowly over their faces.

Rob D'you want a drink of anything? Cup of tea?

David Cup of tea would be lovely, thanks. Do you mind if I borrow your loo?

Rob Course. You know where it is?

David Yes, sure.

David exits. Rob puts the kettle on and gets out a teapot with a tea cosy and two mugs, and makes a pot of tea.

While he waits for the kettle, he looks at the tea cosy.
Very slowly, he picks it up and puts it on his head. Stays
like this for a moment. The kettle boils. He takes the tea
cosy off. David enters.

Rob They shouldn't be long.

David Youth theatre, is it?

Rob That's it.

David Looking forward to that.

Rob Yes. I'll let this brew.

David Poppy isn't in it yet though?

Rob No, Fiona just took her to pick up the boys. I just got
back through the door myself.

David I see. How is she now, is she okay?

Rob She's fine, thank you. An amazing recovery, actually.
The doctors say because she's so young she's more likely to
fully recover. The body still has so much time to grow.

David It was a muscular illness, wasn't it.

Rob Nervous system.

David Oh, sorry.

Rob Guillain-Barré. Attacks the nerves so the parts that
control the muscles shut down, and then you can't move.

David I see. Well I'm so glad she's clear of it.

Rob We're very lucky. They tell you not to look it up, but
of course you do, we're online here now so you look it up,
and apparently only fifty per cent of people survive.

David Oh my God.

Rob So the fact she's going to recover completely is –

David I didn't know it was as dangerous as that.

Rob That's why she was so long in hospital, yeah.

David You must have been out of your mind.

Rob I was. And Fiona, obviously it was my first time, but she never had anything like this with the boys, so neither of us knew what to do really.

David You just have to trust the doctors.

Rob That's it. Barney and Josiah were great with her.

David Yes?

Rob We didn't take them to see her too often. Because of school. But she liked seeing her brothers when they came.

David Of course. I am sorry.

Rob Yeah. But it's done now. Shall I pour this tea?

David Thanks.

Rob pours them tea.

Rob How are you anyway, David? Settling in the new place?

David Oh, yes, thanks. Very happily settled. The village is under one of the firing ranges on the Plain, so there's great walking country, as long as there's no shelling practice.

Rob Lovely.

David I think the boys like it. They like Salisbury.

Rob I hope so.

David Good schools.

Rob That's it. What's your nearest town, it's not here, is it?

David I go to Marlborough for shopping.

Rob Nice place.

David It's lovely.

Rob Glad to get out of London?

David I suppose so. I would have liked to find a way to keep the Harlesden house, but I couldn't make it work. And it's good to be able to drive and see the boys.

Rob Yeah.

David I think from London it might have ended up too far. But I'm getting some work down here now. So hopefully soon I won't have to travel quite so often.

Rob Are you in and out a lot?

David A bit.

Rob I'm the same.

David Really?

Rob But the schools.

David That's it.

Rob And abroad?

David Still a bit of that. Less now. There was a time when I was half the year in the US, and that was wonderful, but not for ever. What about Fiona's work, what's she doing?

Rob Oh, she's having a bit of a change actually. She's taken over a community choir.

David How interesting.

Rob It was advertised in the *Journal*, and she thought she'd try it out. Their last conductor had just run off with the money, so they're starting back from nothing, but they pay her every week.

David What sort of repertoire?

Rob Nothing too difficult yet. Not everyone reads music. I think it's starting from a low base and building up, but people like her. She's good at marshalling a horde. Tells a dirty joke every week, all that.

David That's very good.

Rob It would be good if it gave us roots. They shouldn't be long now.

David No.

Rob Sometimes it overruns. Do you know the play they're doing?

David It's *Our Town*, isn't it?

Rob That's it. I don't know it.

David I think I saw it years ago.

Rob Any good?

David If you like endlessly remembering things as they used to be, I suppose it's okay. I am so glad that Poppy's going to be all right.

Rob Thank you. I could never have imagined it. What it was like.

David No.

Rob You think life will be one thing, then it turns into another.

David Indeed.

Rob But she made it. Southampton hospital's a nightmare, though.

David Why was she so far away?

Rob Nearest decent paediatric unit. I hate hospitals. And ambulances, and telephones. You get away with it for so long, but they come for us all in the end. An ambulance will visit every house, and everyone gets a phone call, and we all end up in hospital at last.

David Hopefully she'll have a long time before she's back in one.

A sound offstage.

Sounds like footsteps?

Rob That must be them.

Lights out. When they rise again, David is at the piano.

4

David plays the chords from Britten's 'Moonlight' interlude from Peter Grimes. *When he finishes he closes the lid of the piano, slowly, beautifully, then stands and steps back from the keyboard, and Fiona box-breathes, and then the scene begins.*
Rob and Fiona onstage.

Fiona Take a seat, David.

David All right. Boys at school?

Rob That's it, yeah.

David Good. Everyone okay?

Rob We're fine. Cup of tea?

David I'm fine.

David sits. Everyone is round the table.

Fiona You already know what's happened?

David Barney called me. Barney's been very stupid.

Fiona I think more than stupid.

David Right.

Fiona They've wrecked the house. We were only gone a night. He won't tell us everyone who's been over. He's wrecked his sister's room, someone pulled all the heads off her dolls. The back window's broken.

Rob He hasn't even had the decency to fucking apologise yet.

David Don't speak about my son like that.

Rob Excuse me?

David Don't raise your voice, it's not necessary.

No one speaks for a moment.

You're a part of his upbringing but I'm his father and you don't raise your voice at him in front of me, all right?

Rob All right, David.

Fiona I called you over because you're going to have to take some responsibility here.

David What do you mean?

Fiona He's going to have to stay with you for a bit, all right? We can't have him here right now. We've taken his keys off him, if we can't trust him in our house he'll need to stay somewhere, so you need to step up.

David Sorry, I'm slightly confused, why are you talking to me like this is my fault?

Fiona I'm not saying that. It's very much his fault, and we just don't want him in our house right now.

David Okay. That's fine, obviously.

Fiona Good.

David And how long is this going to last?

Fiona For the time being you just need to take some responsibility for your son.

David Thank you, yes, you've made that very clear. You've called me round here because you want Barney to come and stay with me for a bit.

Fiona Yes.

David Fine. As I've said, that's fine.

David stands.

He can come over whenever he likes.

Fiona What, so you're just going?

David I think so, yes.

Fiona You don't think there are things to talk about?

David It all seems very clear to me. Barney's been an idiot, and hurt you, and now he's coming to stay with me for a bit while everyone calms down. I don't want to stay here while you're angry, and I don't want to get angry myself.

Fiona Off you go again then.

David Right.

Fiona God forbid you ever have to talk about anything.

David Fiona, stop it. When you're ready to have an actual conversation I will have one with you. There's no reason we're not on the same team on this, but you don't want to be, so I'm going.

Fiona When have you ever had an actual conversation?

David Please.

Fiona People think because I'm a fucking woman they can call me emotional, so they don't have to listen to anything I say.

David I'm just saying this doesn't have to be an argument.

Fiona Some conversations are confrontational, David. Sometimes people have to argue a bit. It's not that I get angry, the problem is that you just run away.

David I really don't have to listen to this. I'm going to go.

Fiona And prove my point.

David Do you know what it's like? Being away from them. Knowing they're going on and I'm not here? We'll speak in the week. Goodbye.

David exits.

Fiona (*shouting*) Fuck!

A moment.

Rob What happened then?

Fiona What happened then?

Rob What happened then?

Fiona You didn't feel like speaking up to support me?

Rob Fiona, don't.

Fiona What?

Rob Turn it on me.

Fiona Sorry. I'm sorry. Oh, fuck. It never stops being difficult.

Rob What?

Fiona Having a marriage that stopped.

Rob You okay?

Fiona No. I'm fine, I'm fine. He called me a bully.

Rob No.

Fiona Am I a bully?

Rob Don't think about it. We'll have a week now. Barney can go and live with David for a week, and then we can pick up the pieces. It'll be okay.

Fiona We've done what we needed. Do you think that we've done the right thing?

Rob Well, it's like the French Revolution, isn't it. It's too soon to say.

Lights out.

Act Two

I

*David sits at the piano. He plays the top and bottom notes
in an alternating pattern, the beginning of a warm-up, as
the actors enter the space. Then the lights rise, and Peggy
and Bert stand either side of a barrel organ. Bert begins to
play it. There's a monkey on the front, and a sort of doll.
Bert dances.*

Bert There, that's not bad is it.

David Brilliant.

Bert See the little monkey on the front?

David Yeah?

Bert That's me.

David Why's that you?

Peggy Because contrary to appearances he's actually the
monkey and I'm the organ grinder.

David Very good.

Bert And that there's Lady Gaga.

David Is it?

Bert I thought I'd modernise it a bit.

David Can we see inside?

Bert Oh, no, don't worry about that.

David Why not? I want to see how it works.

Bert I've had to take the parts out.

David Oh.

Bert They broke down, and I couldn't fix it. I can't get my hands to work right any more. It's just a tape recorder in there now.

David Oh right. Well not to worry.

Bert I just can't move my hands right. I'm getting rid of a lot of my tools for the same bloody reason.

David Are you?

Bert The heavy machinery, yeah. No point in it now. So it might as well go to the school, we thought, and they're taking a bit of it. I don't know what we'll do with the rest.

Peggy It upsets us to see it all in the garage not getting used.

Bert It does, yeah.

Peggy A reminder. We have to get old.

David Better than the alternative.

Bert You say that now, you wait and see.

David So how does it work now, then?

Bert I said, it's just a tape. I press play. I only turn the handle for moving the dancers.

David I see. Well that's still very good.

Peggy That's why he did another dancer, isn't it. And he thought a modern one like Lady Gogo would be good.

David It's great. She's really funny.

Bert Do you think so?

David Definitely.

Bert I'm glad. I thought it would interest younger people.

Peggy I might have to sit down, I'm not so good at this standing up any more.

David Of course, sorry. Shall I fix us some tea?

David helps Peggy down. Bert sits down by himself. David remains standing.

Peggy (*as she sits*) I'll help.

David No, don't worry. You sit down.

Bert We take our camping stools when we go and do the fetes.

David Do you still take it out to the fetes?

Peggy For the air ambulance. We don't do the handbells any more but we can still do this.

David Very good. Hang on.

David exits.

Peggy Told you he'd like it.

Bert He's being polite.

David (*off*) Where are your sweeteners, Mum?

Peggy Are they not in the cupboard?

David No.

Peggy They might be by the bread bin.

David Great, thanks.

Enter David. He stays standing.

Be a minute.

Peggy So you said on the phone that Barney had a job now?

David Yes. Sort of.

Bert Why sort of?

David He's assistant director of a play, but he's not being paid for it.

Bert Oh.

David But it's a route to getting paid.

Bert I see.

Peggy Is it a good theatre?

David I think so. One of those ones above a pub.

Peggy Yes.

David But they're moving it to an old library next year.

Bert Do they never have their theatre in a theatre?

Peggy Oh, Bert. They convert them! Put blinds up and the like so that you can have blackouts.

David That's it. I'll just get the tea.

Peggy Thank you.

David exits.

Bert It's not a job if it isn't paid.

Peggy I'm sure that he knows what he's doing.

Bert Life is very short to do things for no money.

Enter David with cups of tea on a tray. He doesn't sit.

David Here we go, everyone.

Peggy Thank you, David.

David Mum, that's you. Dad.

Bert Thank you.

Peggy Lovely.

Bert So what's it about?

David Barney's play?

Bert Yeah.

David Well. He did explain it. There are these people, who meet each other. And they sit around. And then one of them dies. And that's it really . . . It's got songs.

Peggy Sounds great.

Bert So you've got shot of him? I mean he's not living with you any more?

David Well, he's very welcome to come back whenever he needs to.

Bert That's good.

Peggy And Joz is in Norwich, isn't he.

David Yes. First term.

Peggy He's all right, is he? Enjoying himself?

David Yes, all fine so far.

Peggy And how about their mother, how's Fiona?

David Well, fine I think. They're planning on moving.

Peggy Yes? Where to?

David I think they said the Welsh borders, actually. Somewhere around Hay-on-Wye.

Peggy Oh, lovely.

David Not till Poppy's finished school. You know Poppy, their daughter.

Peggy Yes.

David But that's the next thing, I think.

Peggy I see.

Bert All her work's in Salisbury though?

Peggy Yes, but she can start again.

Bert Gets too late to start again at some point.

Peggy Not for her though, she's still young.

David I'm sure they'll make a success of it.

Peggy And what about you, David, things all right with you?

David Oh yes. Doing too much. Teaching too much.

Bert That's always been you.

David But you never know which job might be the one that makes your fortune.

Bert They never come, those.

David No. But it's fun looking for them.

Bert You won't be moving around again and all that, will you? You're set up where you are.

David Yes, I think so. I used to think I wanted to die here, in the house where I was born. Now I think I'll be happy to die in the house where I'm living.

Peggy Funny way of expressing it, but that's good.

David Is it?

Bert Course. It's so well located.

David Yes. And what about you two, have you been all right?

Peggy Oh, well. We're very fortunate. We carry on.

Bert Yes.

Peggy We're very lucky. We get a lot of visitors popping in, and I've got Torch club, and the church, and WI and the Workers' Educational. And we have lots of wonderful memories.

Bert Mm.

Peggy We're not as mobile, and Bert's not enjoyed having to give up driving, have you.

Bert No.

Peggy Like going fast on your scooter to the shops.

Bert Mobility scooter, yes.

Peggy But we're lucky.

David John pops in a lot, doesn't he.

Peggy Oh yes, and Elizabeth over the road.

Bert Every bloody day.

Peggy And we've been very lucky to be able to stay in our home.

Bert Go to the trouble of building it, you might as well stay in it as long as you can.

David Coming up sixty years.

Peggy Yes. And still the same view of the fields and the church out the window. Very lucky. Lots has changed and lots has gone but not that. When I had my job in the poor house there were people just as old as us who lived there.

David That's how you got this place.

Peggy That's right.

Bert And I saved.

Peggy Of course you did, love. But David's right, the money we had from Arthur ran the poor house when he died bought us this field.

Bert But I paid for a lot of the house.

Peggy Of course you did. I ought to think about starting on lunch, really. If that's the time.

Bert It is.

Peggy Well then.

David You okay, Mum?

Peggy Could you give me a hand up?

David helps Peggy up.

David There you go.

Peggy Thank you.

David Why don't I help you in the kitchen?

Peggy Oh, you don't have to.

David Go on, let me.

Peggy No, you keep your dad busy or he'll make mischief.

David All right then. What are we having?

Peggy Well we're having ham, but I'll do Barney something different if he's still vegetarian?

David Barney's not here, Mum.

Peggy Oh yes. That's right. I'd gone out and got special sausages. Ah well.

Peggy exits.

David Nice cup of tea. So you've got a mobility scooter now then?

Bert Oh, yeah.

David Goes fast?

Bert Fast enough. Faster than I can! (*Beat.*) When you think back to years ago, do you get the good things or the bad come to mind?

David Sorry?

Bert She says she gets the happy memories. Not like that for me. I don't like thinking about all that. Because I can't have it again.

David Right.

During this next speech David finds a time to sit.

Bert I think of the war. My brothers who died, my half-brothers on the memorial. In Malaysia I saw a man shot in the head for trying to push into a queue for rations. Officer just walked up to him and shot him like that. No one said anything. When we were bombed coming out of Narvik, I remember I caught the eye of this signalman standing on the same spot as me on a ship we were passing in the harbour mouth. We were looking at each other, like both of us knew what a pickle we were in, and then there was this explosion. I was knocked off my feet. A huge cloud. And when the cloud cleared I looked for him again, and he wasn't there any more. Just a chunk of the ship gouged out where the bomb hit. And even as I saw that, we were hit as well. This bomb landed two feet from me, but it didn't explode. Ripped through the deck. I looked down through the hole to the hold below. When we got back to Scapa Flow, we sailed into a minefield. Magnetic mines. We heard them clamping to the hull and turned the engines off. We didn't know how to get to shore, and then this lieutenant said if they're magnetic mines, we'll be all right on the life rafts, they'll leave them alone. He said he'd jump on a raft, get to shore, and then we'd get everyone else off once we knew it was safe. And the sailor who got told to row him in was a man named Pookie Finn. I knew him a bit. So Pookie and this lieutenant lowered a raft down into the water, and they climbed down. And about twenty feet out, they hit a mine, and this geyser of water shot a hundred foot in the air. That was the last of Pookie Finn. That's what I think about. All the time. Peggy and I went back once. To Narvik. On a cruise. I couldn't stay there. I was shaking.

David All right, Dad.

Bert Anyway. Have I told you we're having a street named after us?

David No?

Bert After my half-brothers.

David Right?

Bert fishes a clipping from his pocket.

Bert They're building a new estate down by the station, and the developers thought to name the roads after names on the memorial.

David That's great.

Bert gets up to take the clipping over to David.

Bert Yes, they did an unveiling. I went along with my medals. It was horrible.

David is looking at the clipping. Bert stands.

David Why?

Bert Oh, I don't know. I suppose I thought. In a few years' time it will be a hundred years since the Great War, and here in this village, if I play my cards right, there'll still be a man living whose brothers were killed in it. Who goes to look at his brothers' names on the memorial. And then before long there won't be anyone any more. There'll be a street with people living on it. People will have their childhood memories of Norris Mews, and that'll be how it goes on, the story. Before long that'll be all there is.

David And us, Dad.

Bert Yes, but you won't live here. I need the loo.

Bert gets up.

David Want a hand?

Bert No, fine. What happened then?

Bert exits. Peggy enters.

Peggy Where's Ivan the Terrible gone?

David Needed the loo.

Peggy Wants all the attention, that one. Silly man. Who'd have thought I'd put up with him all this time? When we had our seventieth anniversary, you remember his speech, he said the secret is trust and understanding. 'She doesn't trust me and I don't understand her.' I thought that was very funny. He doesn't deal as well with our old age. Best to think about what you keep hold of, not what you give away. What happened then? Come on you, come and help me peel these potatoes.

She turns to exit. The lights change, and all the actors enter the space, finding their way to their next positions over the following music.

2

David plays 'What Power Art Thou' from Purcell's King Arthur *on the piano. Rob sings the part. Then everyone is on stage, but only Fiona and Rob are lit. Rob lights a match and lets it burn all the way down before snuffing it.*

Rob I woke up and you weren't there. Can't sleep?

Fiona Sorry.

Rob Why?

Fiona For not sleeping.

Rob What's up?

Silence.

Fiona I miss being a mum.

Rob You still are.

Fiona You know what I mean. Do you know what I mean?

Rob You still are, though.

Fiona But who am I if they've all gone?

Rob Who you always were.

Fiona I never ask myself these questions.

Rob What questions?

Fiona A hundred years ago my family had never even set foot on this island. I never think about it. I remember talking to Peggy about it. David's mum. Her dad came to England the same time as my family.

Rob Where from?

Fiona From here.

Rob From Wales?

Fiona North Wales. He didn't speak English when he got to London. He had to work it all out. And when he was old he forgot all his English again, she said. When he died he only spoke in Welsh. You can't get back to things, you know. You can't get back to anything at all.

Rob It's not about getting back.

Fiona I miss it all.

Rob Do you want a cup of tea or something?

Fiona When we make this move maybe things will be different.

Rob Why?

Fiona I don't want to be here any more. This is the place where I got old.

Rob You're not.

Fiona I need to be at the beginning of something again. How does everyone deal with this? Getting less and less young till you're dead.

Rob Same way you do.

Fiona What?

Rob They just skip a night's sleep now and then, and freak out a bit. Feel their hearts beating in their chests.

Fiona and Rob disappear, still on stage but unlit. Bert is in a wheelchair, and David is beside him. David lights a match and lets it burn all the way down before snuffing it.

David The doctor says you've got a chest infection, Dad.

Bert Oh, God. I'm lying here with this great bloody plank stuck under my back, you won't do anything about it, you just say it's a chest infection, by God.

David You haven't got anything under you, Dad.

Bert By God.

David Is your back hurting?

Bert Course it is, course it is, I've got this bloody, oh. So painful. And you won't do anything about it.

David We're doing everything we can, Dad, we're all doing everything we can.

Bert You haven't been here, you wouldn't know. Oh, this isn't important after all. It's so very sad to learn you're not important.

David Shall we shift you a bit? Would it help if we moved you around?

Bert You can't move me!

David Why not?

Bert They've tied my legs together.

David They haven't, Dad. Come on. Let's at least move your legs shall we?

Bert If you can, I doubt you can.

David starts shifting Bert's legs under the blanket.

I'll lose my bag.

David Just be careful not to.

Bert Oh, how can you say that? Oh, you're so cruel. I can feel it's come away.

David You're all right, Dad.

Bert Never trust anyone in this life.

David Dad.

Bert Where are all the faces round my bedside? Never trust anyone at all. I need a piddle terrible bad.

David It's all right. There we go, what about that, is that better?

Bert I want to lift up my leg.

David If I put a blanket under it?

David picks up a blanket.

Bert Oh, David.

David Where does it hurt?

Bert My back, it's my back, it's my back. I'm going to piddle.

David That's okay.

Bert No, my bag's off.

David It's okay, you're fine.

Bert There, look, I'm piddling. Oh, oh, it's all hot.

David That's just the tube.

Bert It's all down my legs.

David It's just the tube. Do you want some water?

David tries to give Bert a drink.

Bert No no no! You have to lift me up.

David Okay. Shall we try?

David tries to raise Bert. Bert cries out in pain.

Bert Not that. Not that. Oh, what a pickle.

David We can try.

Bert No, it hurts too much, I just won't have any.

David We can do it really gently.

Bert No.

David Come on, we can do it.

David raises Bert up. Bert cries out.

There you go. All right. You're all right.

Bert Oh, that's better. I asked you to do that, didn't I ask you to do that before?

David Now let's have a drink of water.

Bert Thank you.

David gives Bert a drink. This happens very slowly, as if in slow motion.

David There you go. There you go.

Bert That's enough thank you.

David All right. I ought to go and move the car. Only gives you two hours, isn't that terrible?

Bert I'm sorry.

David That's all right.

Bert I'm sorry I'm getting in the way of you moving your car.

David Don't be like that, come on.

Bert Well.

David I'll be ten minutes. And I'll see you when I get back, yeah?

Bert Oh, well. You dream your dreams and I'll dream mine.

David All right, Dad.

Bert Dave?

David Yes?

Bert Don't tell her, will you. Don't tell her what a pickle I'm in.

The lights change, and Peggy is sitting on the other side of the stage. The lights go out on Bert. Bert and Fiona and Rob are, however, still on stage. Peggy lights a match and lets it burn all the way down before snuffing it.

Peggy
'Into my heart an air that kills
From yon far country blows;
What are those blue remembered hills,
What spires, what farms are those?

That is the land of lost content,
I see it shining plain,
The happy highways where I went
And cannot come again.'

You know that I love you, don't you.

David Yes, Mum.

Peggy And you know that I love you so much. And you know that whenever I've got cross it's just because I'm grumpy like everyone else, and I let myself down, like everyone does. And you know that even when I lose my temper I'm still in love with you and I'm only annoyed with myself.

David I know.

73

Peggy Your turn.

David Really?

Peggy Read me a story.

David
>'Softly, in the dusk, a woman is singing to me;
>Taking me back down the vista of years, till I see
>A child sitting under the piano, in the boom of the
>   tingling strings,
>And pressing the small, poised feet of a mother who
>   smiles as she sings.
>
>In spite of myself, the insidious mastery of song
>Betrays me back, till the heart of me weeps to belong
>To the old Sunday evenings at home, with winter
>   outside,
>And hymns in the cosy parlour, the tinkling piano our
>   guide.
>
>So now it is vain for the singer to burst into clamour
>With the great black piano appassionato. The glamour
>Of childish days is upon me, my manhood is cast
>Down in the flood of remembrance, I weep like a child
>   for the past.'

Peggy Oh, that's a good one.

David Yes.

Peggy We were so proud when you won your award. And went to America. When they rang you up. The whole world was yours then. But you can never go back. That's the danger, isn't it. You can't go home. Do you sometimes feel like you're still out there? Sometimes I feel like at the start of my life there must have been this perfect day, and everything since has been a falling away from it. We were together once. Must have been. But now we're all flung into corners. I'm very tired, David. Why do I have to stay here without him?

74

David You didn't, Mum. Not for long. You left as well not too long after. In the hospital. A lot of people came to see you. And then when you were on your own at the end of the day, you went. And the church was so full for you, and the wake was at the Pytchley.

Peggy And you all wore ties to the funeral?

David And I closed all the curtains in the house.

Peggy Then am I here in someone's dream? Someone doesn't want me to have gone.

David My son is writing us.

Peggy Is this Barnaby's project?

David Will you be okay getting to bed?

Peggy Oh, yes. What a lovely day.

David Yes.

Peggy I'm very lucky. Thank you.

David I'll show myself out.

Peggy All right. Drive safe.

David I will. Call you tomorrow?

Peggy All right. Night night.

The lights go out on David, but all four unlit actors are watching Peggy. She reaches up into the air for something, then puts her arm back down and shakes her head fiercely. Then she seems to change her mind, and reaches up in the air again . . .

And the lights go out. When they rise again, the stage is bare. David enters in silence and crosses to the piano, sits down.

3

David plays the opening of the second movement of his Piano Concerto. Then he shuts the lid and turns round.

Fiona, Rob and David are in the garden. Rob is wearing a hat. David picks up a panettone. David whistles a trill.

David Hello!

Rob David, hi.

Rob crosses to David and shakes his hand.

David How are you, Rob?

Rob Really well, thanks.

David Hi, Fiona.

Fiona Hello, David.

David I brought a gift!

Fiona Oh, thanks.

David Panettone, people like panettone.

Rob I love panettone.

David Shall I put it inside?

Fiona Sure. We could have it now?

David If you like?

Fiona The boys are out on a walk, should be home in a minute. We can all have tea.

David Great.

Fiona I'll toast some.

David Mind if I borrow your loo? Long drive.

Fiona Of course, it's through in the back there, on your left.

David Great.

Rob Let me take that for you.

Rob takes the panettone.

David Thanks. One sec.

David exits.

Rob Shall I cut this up and stick it in the grill then?

Fiona Lovely. We'll wrap up for a minute, shall we?

Rob Great.

Fiona I'll make tea. Coffee?

Rob Tea's great.

Fiona You pack the tools up and I'll do that.

Fiona takes the panettone from Rob.

Rob Shall we call the boys?

Fiona Good thought.

Fiona takes out her phone, and makes a call.

Hey Bar, just calling to let you know your dad's here, if you want to head back. Okay. See you both in a bit.

Rob Answerphone?

Fiona Yeah.

Rob They'll pick it up.

Fiona Yeah. One minute.

Fiona exits. Rob takes his hat off. David enters.

David So this is where you are now.

Rob Yes, welcome.

David It's beautiful. Beautiful view.

Rob It is. We're very lucky. The garden now it's spring.

David How are the winters?

Rob Hell.

 David laughs.

David I'm sorry.

Rob Still working out how to survive them. We'll get there though.

David Is it very cold?

Rob Yeah, and there's the rain. We've been snowed in at some point every year so far.

David Really?

Rob That's Wales, apparently. And it's little things. The heating all runs off stoves, so we get through so much firewood, and we have to spend days stacking the deliveries when they come. Days and days, when you add it up. Then you're on your hands and knees getting them going, you know. But there's a pleasure to be taken in that.

David Absolutely.

Rob It was a big thing for Fiona, trying to be more connected to where our energy came from. Where our food came from. And actually, doing the work of heating the house yourself, there is something satisfying in that. Rather than flicking a switch.

David Of course. That track must get tricky.

Rob Turns into a river when it rains.

David Yes. But it's worth it.

Rob It will be once we've fixed the septic tank.

David Oh dear, really?

Rob It's like that when you take over any place, isn't it. And it'll never be finished.

David Everywhere's always falling down really, isn't it.

Rob Some parts just further along than others, but everything's going the same way. How was your journey over?

David Oh, yes, fine.

Rob It's Lincoln you've moved to now, isn't it.

David Lincolnshire, that's right. Just outside Louth. Caroline and I wanted a house big enough to fit all the pianos in, and it turns out the furthest south you can find one on our budget is just outside Grimsby.

Rob Nice part of the world?

David Oh, beautiful. The Wolds. Miles from everywhere, but that's the trade-off.

Rob That's it. And how's it going?

David Gutting the place. Had to redo all the plumbing. And we're replacing the septic tank.

Rob laughs.

Rob Well that makes me feel better, I must say.

David Yes. Do we know how far the boys have gone?

Rob Probably only up to the top field. We've called and left a message to say you're here.

David Oh good. Just that I'm rehearsing from three, so I won't be able to stay all that long I'm afraid.

Rob Oh right.

David Sorry.

Rob No, don't be silly. It's great you can see the place.

David How long have you been here now?

Rob This is our third spring.

David Is it really? I didn't realise it had been so long.

Enter Fiona.

Fiona Here we go, panettone and tea.

David Marvellous.

Fiona Barney called back, they'll only be a minute, so I made enough for five.

Rob Great.

Fiona We'll leave that to brew for a minute shall we? Butter if you want it.

Fiona Barney called back, they'll only be a minute, so I made enough for five.

Rob Great.

Fiona We'll leave that to brew for a minute shall we? Butter if you want it.

They sit down around the garden table.

David Not for me thanks.

Rob I'll have a bit.

Rob and Fiona butter their panettone, while David eats his. Fiona holds a mug up to the light, checking whether it's clean.

Fiona So here we are! What do you think of it?

David I was just saying, I think it's absolutely wonderful. A wonderful location.

Fiona Isn't it? We'll show you round the house when we've had our cake. It's a bit of a mess at the moment.

David eats some panettone.

David This is quite good, isn't it?

Fiona Lovely. Shall I pour the tea?

Fiona pours the tea.

Rob Great. So what is your gig tonight, David?

David Oh, just some English stuff. Sullivan. In the church at the edge of Hay, you know it?

Rob Oh yeah.

David Nice place.

Rob Is it? I don't think I've been in.

Fiona I've done a gig there.

David Have you?

Fiona With one of my choirs. Lovely acoustic for singing. Bit rich for piano.

David Is it?

Fiona There we go.

Fiona hands them tea.

David Thanks so much.

Rob Lovely.

David Well. You really have run for the hills, haven't you.

Fiona We have. All the kids gone. I feel like I've got my life back.

David Really?

Fiona I just felt as if for years I hadn't done anything.

Rob But now you are.

Fiona Now we are, yes. How's your place, is that going all right?

David Oh, yes, thank you. I was just saying to Rob, there's a lot of work to do.

Fiona And how are things going with Buckby, what's happening with that?

David Oh, well, we've got a buyer. So it's just a case of getting all that through.

Fiona Has there been a lot of paperwork?

David John's doing most of it, so I can't complain.

Fiona It's very strange to think of it going. And whoever buys it will change it. I suppose you won't ever want to go past.

David I don't think I'll have any reason to really. Besides visiting them. They're in the churchyard of the Baptist chapel. In the grave of Bert's parents.

Fiona That's lovely. It was a very beautiful service.

David Yes. Thank you.

Fiona I'm sorry I didn't go to Bert's.

David That's all right.

Fiona At the time I just felt like it wasn't my place to. You know. And I thought of him, of course, because they were always so good to me, but I felt I might be intruding. Then after I'd gone to Peggy's, I felt like I should have been at both.

David It's all right.

Fiona How have you been?

David Well, I don't know. It's strange, isn't it. You don't know how to feel. It's harder for John really. He was there every day with her, having her lunch. I don't know how to express how I feel about it really. I try not to think about it all too much.

Fiona No?

David I just don't like to be always looking backwards. I'm interested in what's happening next.

Fiona I know what it feels like. Going on without them. Knowing they've vanished and you're still here.

David Yes. The one thing I did do after Mum died, I went round and looked at the places we'd been.

Fiona Did you?

David The Watling Street farm and the little chapel at Norton where my grandfather used to preach. And the house where Mum was born in Drayton. And I went up the top of Borough Hill, where they used to farm a hundred years ago. Where all the hedges must have been laid by my grandfather. The cottage is gone now, there's just a cleft in the hillside where it used to be, but by its side there's a monkeypuzzle that was there when they were. You can see it in the photos. I went and looked at that, and thought of them. Then I went back down the hill, down the little track where Mum and Dad first bumped into each other. And I thought, that's enough of that, I think.

A moment. Rob puts his hat back on.

Well then. How about a tour of the house?

Lights out. When they rise, Fiona, Rob and David are standing together.

Fiona, Rob and David onstage. They sing the end of 'The Long Day Closes'. Then they part, and behind them, one last time, we see . . .

Peggy and Bert are waving from the window of their sitting room as David pulls away. When Bert stops, Peggy's arm stays reaching in the air for a moment, then drops.

Bert There he goes.

Peggy Yes.

Bert Seems all right.

Peggy He does. And the boys.

Bert Who'd have thought it, eh? On and on. Tired now. Might shut my eyes for a minute.

Peggy That's a good idea.

Bert Shall we have a sit-down?

Peggy Go on then.

Bert There we go, love.

Bert helps Peggy sit down.

Peggy Thank you.

Bert That's all right. Is the washing-up done?

Peggy David did it.

Bert Oh, he won't have done it right.

Peggy Well, that's all right. We can always do it again later. He seems all right.

Bert Yes.

Peggy I think we did just fine. When you think of where we started. We stopped and looked at an old Anderson shelter the other day, with Torch club.

Bert Oh yeah?

Peggy There are lots of them still on allotments. And they drove us over to see. I suppose they thought we'd be interested. I suppose we were.

Bert Bloody things.

Peggy Yes, but I didn't like to see them all rust. We came up out of those in the mornings with nothing, not even knowing if the house was still up. We came out of those and started again. I don't know what became of that. Do you know, I think I might go up to bed. Will you help me back up? Sorry.

Bert Course.

Bert gets up and helps Peggy up.

Peggy Thank you.

Bert Okay.

Peggy What about you?

Bert I might do the same.

Peggy I do like nodding off, it's the loveliest. 'They lay down and accepted the gift of sleep.'

Bert What's that?

Peggy From the *Odyssey*.

Bert Is it now?

Peggy It is.

Bert How do you know that?

Peggy I read it.

Bert You read it?

Peggy Where do you think all the young ones get their brains from?

Bert You're a dark horse, you.

Peggy Not just a pretty face. And if you hadn't found me at Waterloo station, I'd have got that carpet home as well.

Bert I bet you would.

Peggy I'd have just asked some other handsome man to help me.

Bert Oh, now. Pass up on a catch like me?

Bert dances for Peggy.

Peggy I liked it better when we still shared a bed.

Bert Yes.

Peggy But the way we wake up in the night. I think we'd both be long dead from lack of sleep if we were inflicting that on each other.

Bert I reckon so.

Peggy If you could walk back into the past and be at the start of our lives again, would you want to? Would it feel like going home?

Bert Come on, you. Up to bed.

Peggy Mind if I lean on your arm? I think my leg's gone to sleep.

Bert All right.

They start to leave. The lights build, the light on them becomes brighter and narrower.

Peggy
'You have been mine before,
How long ago I may not know:
But just when at that swallow's soar
Your neck turned so,
Some veil did fall –'

Peggy laughs.

Now how does the rest of it go?

Lights out.

End.